Cleave

Poems

Darla Himeles

Copyright © 2021 by Darla Himeles

All rights reserved. No part of this book may be reproduced in any manner without written consent except for the quotation of short passages used inside of an article, criticism, or review.

Get Fresh Books Publishing, A NonProfit Corp.
PO BOX 901
Union, New Jersey 07083

www.gfbpublishing.org

ISBN: 978-1-7345802-3-5
Library of Congress Control Number: 2021931675

Cover image: "Everything Is the Root" by Dawn Surratt
Cover design & book layout: Sara Pinsonault
Author photo: Robin Miller Photography

Acknowledgements

Some of these poems have appeared, sometimes in slightly different versions, in the following publications:

5 AM: "Burst" & "GODildo"
Atticus Review: "I Tell Anne Sexton about My Uterus"
Bayou Magazine: "What It Felt Like"
Eclipse: A Literary Journal: "Cousin" & "Kiss Me"
Great River Review: "For the FedEx Guy"
NAILED Magazine: "Tony the Cat," "Breach," "Still Your Hand," "Poem to My Therapist about the Abyss," & "Prayer for a Marriage"
Naugatuck River Review: "North Roxbury Drive"
New Ohio Review: "Chino, California"
Off the Coast: "Ferning" (2013) & "Berth" (2016)
Pittsburgh Poetry Review: "In the Beginning" & "Pregnancy Magazine Babies"
Spillway: "Geology Lesson"
Talking River: "Philadelphia"
The Massachusetts Review: "Pigs That Ran Straightaway into the Water, Triumph Of"
The Night Heron Barks: "In the Middle Of"
WomenArts Quarterly Journal: "Home"
Women's Review of Books: "Instructions from My Father"

"Dawn after Maine Votes Yes on Question 1, Repealing Same-Sex Marriage" appears in *Passion and Pride: Poets in Support of Equality* (Moon Pie Press, 2012).

"Conception Poem: Spring" appears in *The Lake Rises* (Witness Post/Stockport Flats, 2013).

"Santa Monica Pier, May 2014" appears in *Voices from Here 2* (The Paulinskill Poetry Project, 2017).

"Miriam, I remember," "Cousin," & "In the Beginning" appear in the chapbook *Flesh Enough* (Get Fresh Books, 2017).

"I Tell Anne Sexton about My Uterus" was selected by Aimee Nezhukumatathil as honorable mention in *Atticus Review*'s 2018 poetry contest.

for my wife, Betsy

Contents

The Self in Transit	1

1

Home	2
What It Felt Like	4
Clip	6
Tony the Cat	8
Goldfinch	9
North Roxbury Drive	10
Claremont, California, 1989	11
Pigs That Ran Straightaway into the Water, Triumph Of	12
Chino, California	13
In the Beginning	15
Breach	16

2

Geology Lesson	18
Burst	20
Topanga	21
GODildo	23
Prayer for a Marriage	24
Kiss Me	25
Cousin	27
Dawn After Maine Votes Yes on Question 1, Repealing Same-Sex Marriage	28
Still Your Hand	29

3

For the FedEx Guy	30
Conception Poem: Spring	32
Poem with First Line by Jean Valentine	33

I Tell Anne Sexton about My Uterus	34
Ferning	35
Insemination 12	36
Little Blue	37
Pricked / A Day in the Life of TTC	38
Loss	39
The inconceivable	41
American As Apple Pie	42
Pregnancy Magazine Babies	43

4

Instructions from My Father	44
Santa Monica Pier, May 2014	46
Marriott Hotel, Marina del Rey	47
Among the Things I Haven't Asked My Father Because I Love Him	48
Philadelphia	49
In the Middle Of	50
Another Woman Shoved Down to the Gravel	51
Miriam, I remember	52
Berth	54
At Framwellgate Bridge	55

5

Poem to My Therapist about the Abyss	56
Still Trying	57
Dear One	58

&

Poem for Evelyn	59
Notes	67
Gratitude	68

The Self in Transit

I turn, pretzelled with pillow,
tray table rattling,

the brass handle
of a hardwood door & open it

between the eyes centered in the brain
& the sun-bled orange behind drawn eyelids;

transparent, childhood's home thickens,
solidifies, & my skirted self enters,

a mud-footed, old-souled child, 1984;
I proceed ten parquet paces, kneel

before the yellow wraparound couch
where I peeled grapes beneath blood-lusty

arrows they flung; I hum
a little *Fiddler*, a little "Dayenu," & this

I swear: my chest pain sings
the sprout of new ventricles;

my nausea, the sudden flurry
of irises blooming at every house I ever loved;

& as I open my eyes' old windows,
the flight lands like dust.

1

Home

Home, I have always wanted you
to bear tomatoes
clambering cages, ballooning life

into open air—
tomatoes juicy and oblong, or round,
heirlooms all sizes,

green, gold, orange, purple;
I have always wanted
to bury my face

in their wetness, feel the leaves
and green arteries cool against
forehead and neck, smell the thick

breath of salsa, marinara, bruschetta.

Home, your smoky scaffolding,
your ghost gardens
where I have placed and plucked palm trees,

the drive sometimes lined in *Washingtonia robusta*,
aloe, *Rosa rugosa*, lavender, lily-of-the-valley,
blueberry, dandelion, lupine—

Down a Maine dirt road, pine and cedar,
a suburban Philly road, elm and maple,
down a row-homed road, a brownstoned road,

a Texas farm road, California beach road,
mountain road, apartment road, mansion road,

six-lane highway, secret passageway—

Home, I dream your driveway, garage, public lot,
curb spot; your metal doorknob, wood, plastic;
your front room's wide-planked floor,

linoleum, marble, oriental rug; here's
your kitchen, basement, library, shower;
your rooms flicker between few and many, old and new,

furnished and empty; and my arousal comes and goes
like tomatoes, from pointy flowers to rotten fruit,
or as you do—or is it me?—always turning, leaving,

storeys expanding, contracting,
the crumpling and un-crumpling duffle bags,
the rain washing, dirtying windows.

Home, I have always wanted you,
a steady place between seed and wilt,
but we just keep squirming every which way, home.

What It Felt Like

Chipping on serrated steel, the bone
was all I heard despite Dad's opened mouth
or what must have been

Mom's bloody screech,—elongated
purple ribbons of her breath. I saw her
body arch back, pause, and flip forward:

the pink robe pooled below as she rose
to her toes, then up further, naked,
the knife between her breasts turning,

and she started spinning too, face down, helicoptering.
I could not believe her limbs
sawed open the ceiling,

her pink body whisked up like paper,
or how the sky was like any other night's
but different, of course, through the kitchen—

and surrounded by plaster, shingles, wet leaves,
my father held the plastic fallen
ring that had surrounded the light fixture

above the counter. He knelt, kissed
and kissed its plastic, did not see
or hear my four-year-old feet run

with baby Darren through the front door
to climb into Mom's car,
ride with her ghost

to the motel, pray to the streaked stars,
promise never to tell, pretend
she was still alive, and well, and my mother.

Clip

Darren, age three,
spins nickels
on the parquet floor
in big wobbly circles,
as I, age six, build
castles out of Vanessa's
baby bottles. Nickels
flick from his fingers
mechanically, their
sound smothered
under Dad's curdled
curses, Mom's loud
whispers, sudden
screams. I turn
finally from his
nickels, my castle,
find my mother
crouched, head
clutched, heaving,
my father gripping
a fist of her
now-detached
hair—a blond nest
he shakes, threats still
streaming from his
cracked voice.
Turning back,
I lunge to where

Darren plunges
a nickel into his wet
mouth, face darkening
to violet—Mom's
shaking him
upside down,
Dad's slapping
his back, when
the nickel tumbles
through spit
to the floor.

Tony the Cat

Against the garage door hurled
Tony like a javelin, in his tuxedo
coat, with his animal shriek, a body
Dad could twist in his hands,
a soft body, proxy for Mom's—
or mine, maybe, if his rage had ever
been tempted. Tony survived,
as did we all somehow, before disappearing
like three dogs before him, no matter
how many fliers Mom and I stapled
to telephone poles, no matter how many
shelters we entered, begging.

Goldfinch

A goldfinch bounds down to the concrete field,
nosing florets, feeding on seeds, as I pace
the cracked schoolyard track. Far away, metal gate,
my mom leaps and blows kisses like a woman

scissored out from a storybook—black and gold jacket,
cherry-red nails, sky-blue shadow. A woman once
clobbered and cut in the kitchen of a house with not enough
locks and too many windows—I still hear the shriek of glass

and speak its broken language—she leaps, waves two-armed,
and blows kisses. I wave back low, stomach level,
wondering *is* she crazy? my gaze blurring toward wings
in ragged greenery beneath the schoolyard fence.

Cheeks hot, belly shimmering from olive to gold,
I am then feathery, limbs streaking ebony, new muscles
tingling—impossibly floating toward the gate.

North Roxbury Drive

Mail lies scattered beneath the slot;
we gather it while separate TVs blare,
carry it up the winding stair, into
the master suite, past the sunken bath
and lit vanity, into the closet as large
as my room. Mom crouches beneath
my stepfather's urn, surrounded by papers.

* * *

On cool tile by the sliding glass door,
she smiles through her news—
an accounting job at a pillow plant!
She can return the suit bought
for interviews. Soon we'll have allowances
again; she'll get dental work done.
All the same, the bank demands eviction.

* * *

We meet in the kitchen before school.
Mom calls the office, reports our absence;
leans forward, arms flattened on the counter;
she exhales in spurts beside twenty boxes
of trash bags and a case of bottled juice.

We line up our bags outside.
No time to sort, just stuff.

Triple-bag, rubber band, tape, shut.

Claremont, California, 1989

On donut days Dad would smack lips, rhapsodize
      between coffee sips
           about what he'd do with a million bucks:

candy-apple red Porsche, Rolex watch,
      modern Venice boardwalk beach house
           at which tourists would gawk.

Nearby bullet claps cranked shoulders to ears
      in that chipboard apartment, but he'd pass a bear claw,
           say *could have been fireworks.*

Strained throat clears, rhythmic wrist twists: those ticks
      picked up in jail all stilled
           when he one day mounted a chair

on the brown stucco landing
      to lift & balance a twig-woven nest
           between thumbs & fingertips.

We kids gathered beneath in bike shorts & wonderment,
      holding breath. His foot slipped,
           a split-second blip—

the nest tipped eggs to pavement.
      All cracked. This was the first time,
           in memory, my dad wept.

Pigs That Ran Straightaway into the Water, Triumph Of

When Jesus casts demons into pigs,
they leap from steep banks

to sea. Some translations suggest
lake. The water, salt or fresh,

muffles a mania of snouts.
The pigs drown. He is the lord

I will never understand
through human stories.

In Cara's photograph, newborn
piglets suckle a Vermont sow.

The sow gives of her flesh
in dappled sunlight.

She is clean & wise & noble,
& her babies number seven, oh holy.

No god would throw demons
upon her. No god would send such beauty

to drown.

Chino, California

Between the outer and inner fences
two crows claw down to cement—

beaks like swords, backs slick,
slashing wings and talons.

I watch them fight from my car today
as I watched my parents as a child: clutching

a book in my lap. I cannot read
the crows or my father, for whom I wait

in my locked car, his bag of belongings
in the back seat beside the maps I printed

to find him. At once, a line cuts
from one building to another: orange

jumpsuits shocking under smoggy, industrial sky.
I pinch my lip, examine their faces, their gaits.

*Not my father, not my father—maybe? No,
not my father.*

Hours pass, the crows disperse.
The prison yard empties.

Two hours after the designated release, a small
group of men gathers at the gate.

Escorted by officers, they wear stiff beige chinos,
white canvas loafers, and baggy T-shirts

to greet the other side. I see him
shaking his gray head to an officer: *No,*

there's nobody here for me—must be a mistake—
Sir, I need the bus fare you promised me.

In the Beginning

The longer your beard, the softer
I heard your father's voice
as he finger-brushed your hair,
eyes closed, tickling your
mother's belly while you,
tiny astronaut, slept amid
her body's stars. I believe
in the beginning, how it is
always shuffling backward,
how every brittle thing softens
in reverse. This fig leaf, stiff
as paper, once knew how to be
small, potential, a speck of star.

Breach

Trust your stomach and thighs'
clenching.   That dank room
with its round bed and too-small
window births only dead-end
flashbacks: self as teenage
Olympia with choker and pinched
nipples, a hollowed peach-fuzz
belly into which he pours molten
wax.   Into which he
pours and pours. Frosted window
glass, the light murky and viscous.
Billy Idol's "White Wedding"
floods the parentless   air, body
bent, then, like a seven. Maybe
what happens next must. And so
the breach   will spasm for years.
And so the mind will blank behind
the dungeon door thrust shut. No
lover will glance   that tender skin
without your legs and back jerking.
You buck   cloven-hooved,
then fawn, eyelashes slow through
hyperventilation, face and feet numb.
Fourteen years old, your puffed eyes
trace stucco constellations. Child,
you've done nothing wrong.

Here: climb those dusty milk crates. Slip
this way   (deep breath)
beneath   window glass.
No ears   can hear or
eyes grip   us. It's been
twenty-   three years.
Wait 'til   you see how
our some   -day beloved's
slick hands   knead cocoa
butter into   our cracked
soles, how   breezes blow
crisp, sweet,   through our
future rooms—vanilla, coffee, lavender—

2

Geology Lesson
for Betsy

Lock the door twice
to show me your maps

and run my fingers
over ancient faults,

tectonic formations.

Hum me these worlds
through the thick

warmth of aged papers
and your buttery scent.

My focus on your lesson
won't stop

the wanderlust
informing my touch.

I am here and I want you

to lay me down on hand-
colored outcrops and deposits,

lift my shirt over my head,
and paint new geologic features.

Sink in this flesh of etched paths
to see if you can stand

its history. Then teach me—
give me your key—

I must collaborate
in this cartography.

Burst

Who wouldn't touch
such sweetness? The bunched silk
of hillocks, mountains,
tangled threads of rivers,
farms like woven potholders—
scenes a body mid-air between homes
could fall into.

And the wing's seductions,
how it begs me to break
glass, climb onto
its gleaming bed, beckon
my lover—how we'd strip
and allow the wind to vacuum
the whole plane toward us.

I'm a mouse with ginger ale and pen,
strapped tightly in.
But my inner hands twist
15C's wavy hair, caress 8D's bare
infant head, unclasp
my lover's bra, rip through denim—
every finger a rose bud, swollen.

Topanga

I drive here with lovers
    when I seek silence.
        And the golden hour lavished
        on these canyons and shrubs
    never fails me.
The road always twists
    this close to the edge
        and each time, the gasp—
        And each time, I caress
    my radio dial like a cheek
as Steve Miller sings
    of those peaches
        shaking on the tree.
        Lovey dovey, lovey dovey,
    just short of swerving
just short of colliding—

Sometimes I lead lovers over
    the mountain to the valley;
        sometimes I park them
        on the shoulder for wind-
    swept viewing; sometimes
my hand grasps a hand.

And when one autumn you led me
    to the park where we'd once been
        hiking, I knew you were on to me
        and I liked it.
    Sun beat like August.

Dust clouded our feet like slippers.
    You brought me down
        a thin path in dry grass
        and around a bend to willow.
    There you undressed me
and all of Topanga
    could hear me singing.

GODildo

I put you in when I want to.
I grip you like a stick shift.
I control my breathing.
I plunge you in and rip you out
like laundry in a bucket.
You hide in the closet.
You smell sweet, like me.
You pretend you love me,
but I could never love you,
oh phallus, oh needy, oh moody one.
Tongueless, mindless, heartless—
you're wholly plastic, wholly function.

Do I praise that you don't abandon me,
non-biodegradable imposter of a dick?
I praise my lover inside me, rocking
my hips with her nibbles and licks.

Prayer for a Marriage
    after Steve Scafidi

When we are old, hunched and softened
by time's loose fingers, may hunger throb
its sore muscle a random Tuesday
afternoon and keep us from dinner plans
with friends. May day darken
around our graze-and-grab-happy
hands, whose secret knowledge blushes us
even then. May the rhinoceros
in your pelvis bruise mine into sunset
and our penguin-fingers fly slick
underwater. And may we kiss
in the open street, three hours late,
before swaying our wearied bodies to eat.

Kiss Me

kiss me on the sidewalk why don't you
kiss me at the market or at least at the car
kiss me at the golf course and oh
for the summer people, kiss me good and hard

kiss me at the chapel
kiss me chewing apple
kiss me on Pride's biggest float

kiss me for the children
kiss me when I never listen
kiss me when I beg and when I don't

kiss me on my father's boat, kiss me
on the front lawn, kiss me
on the bus from Bangor to Boston

kiss me on Cadillac Mountain
kiss me at the downtown fountain
kiss me on the rim of Topanga

kiss me on the throat and kiss me
on the cheek and kiss me
on the lips while I speak

kiss me with a wild tongue
kiss me like a virgin
kiss me like I'm dying in your arms

kiss me for the born agains
kiss me while they mourn our sin
but you'd better never fail to kiss me
out of fear or fear of scorn

Cousin

You will never rip apart the challah,
warm and wrapped in Malaysian linen,

while my wife holds the other end
in our home.

When we met, your back
locked; between your vertebrae

are traditions I have craved,

secretly kissing mezuzahs in doorways
and stumbling through the sh'ma alone.

Our pots and pans are spoiled, cousin, with sins
I don't believe in, and when I bleed,

I touch everything.

Dawn After Maine Votes Yes on Question 1, Repealing Same-Sex Marriage

Bangor Daily News folded, I witness
moonset over the cove,
orb giving itself to horizon.

No sunlight warms the throat
into a hum
as moon falls.

No courthouse, no protest,
no candles, just
moonset over the cove.

Moon keeps on shifting
each day on the line,
staring differently into the light.

Still Your Hand

Another drawn-blinds Saturday
when the slits of my light-
sensitive eyes blur

Zebras in dry grass
become hair across your face

Somewhere a hand whispers
to my leg to stay still

Here   I slip in and out of sleep

Sticky lips   barely shut
whistle lightly

      as a wrecking ball splits
      the walls, the bed,
      forcing our bodies
      beneath our house,
      smashing us with soil-
      infused concrete chunks

and still your hand
upon my leg

the light making hair of grass

your lips lifting sweat
as if we are safe

3

For the FedEx Guy

Oh warrior of ice and snowbanks, trouper
of duty and pride, how timely this delivery
despite your quarter-mile hike up my drive.

You say I'll have to sign for it and hope
I'm warm inside. You say the weather
will change tonight—you are my prophet, dear

FedEx guy. You pass the box with a shrug
to which I dare not reply. If only you knew
what millions were frozen inside. If only

you knew what you carried, Mr. FedEx guy. *Come
inside*, I say to the box as you stride
safely beyond my voice. *Have a seat.* There

once was a man called 5549, lover of art
and sport, teacher and fire dancer, a man
of good genetic line, who walked

into a Pasadena health clinic. Yes, 5549
was used to the protocol but still double-checked
the lock before opening *Playboy* or *Playgirl*

and cradling the plastic cup that caught his white
gold to be whisked away and locked up,
twice tested for all conceivable diseases,

and divided into vials, you wouldn't believe
how small. And when I called, after digesting
the online catalog, requesting one vial of 5549,

the woman said *yes, yes, yes* just like that,
and all women said *yes* then, and my belly
fluttered. From hand to hand to hand,

van to plane to truck, hand to hand again
my millions of motile swimmers have landed
here. Thank you, FedEx guy, for shepherding

my little men all the way to Maine; I'll take
it from here, with my wife, needleless
syringe, and four slippery thighs.

Conception Poem: Spring

We sparked through windows:
two breasted bodies making love

with syringes and welding gloves.

Sweat glistened on Mama B's arms
and my belly

free-fell through the bed.

Ovum, as you left the pod,
my finger traced paths above.

You bobbed in my narrows,

waited for a swimmer
to fuse with you.

Early May, I held my arms

for your imagined weight,
didn't know you had fallen,

ghost speck in blood.

Poem with First Line by Jean Valentine

I saw my soul become flesh,
if you will allow that water
spiders are more than crunch,
fling, and whirr, but bodies
too, fleshy, the way they
scoot with their whole hearts
and splay in the contemplative
pose of flying squirrels
calmly airborne between trees,
though this water spider
was, of course, below the trees,
and amid the fallen trees, mostly
oaks, flicking about on a pond
too murky to swim in. And each
of her legs, if you will allow
her to be female, imprinted
on the water's surface, tracing
tiny o's where feet would be,
and the o's were flickering
with light from the late afternoon
sun—flicking and flickering,
my soul, just then, become flesh.

I Tell Anne Sexton about My Uterus

Everyone in me was a bird
those months I'd palm my belly
& hum down the lane,

but when they'd die, my uterus
would purge their blood

in clumps, brittle ribs & feet
filling the sad menstrual cup,
feathers smearing toilet paper

at night. Each month I assembled
bird scraps in jewelry boxes. Some

I buried in Witherle Woods,
some I burned in beach bonfires,
& others I dried on the deck

to build dream catchers with.
I'd beat all my wings to beckon

back birds each month, poised,
like you, to praise the cells
their triumphant flurry,

but then out would slip a broken beak,
a smear of brown-red feathers.

Ferning

Two white wooly worms stretch and pinch
the length of the deck. Pretend wings happen;
pretend there are no mothballs left. Pretend
the doe hunter did not scout last night in fatigues
on the abandoned property to the west.

Yesterday, four goldfinches, two dull, two light,
pecked at drying-out goldenrod ten happy minutes.
For forty-one days, do not eat from the cow's teat,
or the goat's or the sheep's; let lie the hen's
unfertilized dreams; leave the bubbled eggs of fish,
turn from pork bone marrow and all slaughtered flesh.

Here in the four o'clock sun, *lift her up*. I breathe into
my uterus, internal cavern of inter-clasped palms
poised for whistling (if only it were that easy): puckered lips,
airflow, song. Lift up dull birds and their mates,
does, moths—all who breathe, let's. For eighty-two days,
eat of succulent coconuts, acorn squash, Ida reds.

The harvest moon lights the knife that peels and cores
for applesauce, red, Grandma Ida, like your hair
I never touched, the pink of palms in sunlight,
the uterus if she were cut, the doe shot, the deck's rust.
Lift her up is my song, expanding in moonlight,
the unfurling of one million fiddlehead fern fronds.

Insemination 12

Laid on vinyl and foam-
cushioned table, I tilt pelvis,
legs veed toward white coat sleeves,
graze wet fingertip
over left nipple

and moisten: latex fingers, glisten
of stainless speculum, plastic shaft
unsheathed, vial unscrewed,
cream sucked,
plunger thrust—

Oh baby!
Oh baby, please!

Little Blue

Rise up,
little blue line—
stop hiding.

Drink my amber,
little stick
of maybe.

Little blue,
if you'll come,
I'll praise

& name you,
little sign
of mercy.

Pricked / A Day in the Life of TTC

1.
Another sore vein needled
to measure estradiol, luteinizing hormone, progesterone,
before the condomed ultrasound wand penetrated
to render follicle size, uterine lining—

2.
Collapsed in recliner,
I smiled as Billy acupunctured
hands, arms, shins, feet, ears, forehead, scalp,
just in case—

3.
I gripped the syringe of follicle-stimulating hormone,
pink tile bathroom, Brandi Carlile soundtrack,
pinched belly fat, hovered syringe above flesh,
pierced, breathed, and plunged clear liquid in—

Another faint bruise blushed under skin

Loss

Find an unbroken shell—
        horseshoe crab, Scotch bonnet,

or a doll's head, seaweed tangled
        through hair,

faded plastic irises, sticky grains
        in acrylic lashes,

half buried in sand.
        All matter crumbles,

returns. Even the unborn
        particles of dreams.

*   *   *

Loss pulls blood
        from feet

to clavicles;
        legs drain,

buckling. Lungs
        swell, stiffen;

eyes close,
        barren.

*   *   *

Loss magnifies the sting
 of wind-thrust sleet,

yet insulates—
 wooden hands, arid tongue,

cottony brain.
 Cracked bonnets

reemerge
 limestone

—or some other way.

The inconceivable

knocks around my body
in crimson,

has names I cannot tell.

A Syrian baby
lay tummy down in the sand,
dead in the surf,
his pink body,
his red shirt.

The photo was staged.

He was my nephew
sleeping, my own son
I try sometimes to birth.

American As Apple Pie

Each autumn migrant laborers still handpick most apples, two or three per hand, dozens of handfuls per minute, Spanish ballads & mariachi dancing the leaves. Our only native variety, the crabapple, attracts no such music. No metaphor can undo this. Apples belong to the rose family, their blossom Michigan's state flower. All 50 states grow apples now, over 2,500 varieties. When we slice apples for our children, we cut out the seeds. A person named Isaac cuts apple seeds from red delicious, most boring & popular of American apples, for his sons & young daughter in El Paso as you read this. His trunk bends over paring knife, soap-cleaned fingers, bland flesh with garish skin. He knifes the seeds from each slice in a smooth crescent like his father did & his grandmother, all born in Texas. The onyx seeds he tosses in the trash with some flesh still attached. He sits down with the slices & his children day after day, a ritual before work at ICE, where sometimes his boss assigns him to cut children from parents, throw them in separate cans, kick their heads in, witness a child deliver a stillborn child, here, in Texas, in the United States, after hours of her unanswered cries. No metaphor can undo this. You would not say Isaac "lost" the seeds, even after his wife hauled the garbage bag to the alley garbage bin, even after the garbage carrier dumped the bin's contents into the trash compactor, even when the truck slid the compacted trash into the landfill, even when the city draped the landfill with sod, even after the landfill seeped into the soil. You would say Isaac threw them away.

Pregnancy Magazine Babies

Have you seen, glossy dears,
my daughter? She was sitting
in my lap just yesterday,
a sand-filled balloon. I scratched
her head with feathery fingers,
traced her secret name before she
evaporated into milky breath.

Faces: chocolate, carnelian, ivory, olive:
show me my son, who shook my wrist
as a cat swats string in moonlight.
I followed him with heavy eyes,
hypnotized by the muscle of his crawling.
I kissed his almost-invisible cheek,
but like hair in the pond, he vanished.

Which of you is my child? You, sleeping
in some other woman's sling,
have never known my breast. You,
pawing the mobile in the yellow nursery,
were not my little sandbag, were not
my little cat. I will do whatever you say
if you give me my child. I will nurse
even if it hurts, I will stroller her around
national parks, I will sing him love
songs. I will carry a seven-inch knife,
I will wear pink skirts, anything to bring
her home hear his laugh feel her toes
let him break my heart.

4

Instructions from My Father

Look, hang up and go play Beethoven's third symphony,
second movement, the first several minutes,
and report back. I'm sure it will
convince you. There's beauty in this world,
see, but also anger. Stop making that face—
I can almost hear the disdain. Just listen. It's all there.

Then think of violence. Let your mind go there.
Picture being stalked. The news gives a medley
of examples: girl's body in the river, bloated face,
sonofabitch out of there in minutes
while her family scours her street, her world,
searching. When the cop explains, they'll

sob on camera: *How could this happen?* Will
you listen now? I can help you pay for it. There
are ranges and classes all over the world
where you can learn to shoot in rhythm
with other bright people like yourself. Minutes
after even one lesson, you'll feel safe, you'll face

the darkness with new confidence, face
yourself with new pride. The logistics will
be a no brainer. Just spend a few minutes
finding a spot in the kitchen—somewhere there,
in your cutlery drawer, say, silent
beside your steak knives. Whenever in this world

you hear something, it'll be close. The world
is steeped with psychotic creeps, Darla. Faced

with the prospect of two women sleeping in harmony,
they'll think *This is too good, too easy*. They will!
So bring it to bed, put it in a bedside drawer there.
If a sicko calls your bluff, he's dead in minutes—

or at least wounded. The ritual takes two minutes
from drawer to drawer. No more idealistic shit. World
War II taught us to know better. There, there.
Goddamnit, don't be afraid of it. Dry your face.
I know you're no victim, but men have incredible will.
Life ain't a moonlit stroll after a night at the symphony.

I wish I were there to look into that stubborn face.
Think about it a few minutes? It's your life, your world.
You'll do what you want. At least play the symphony.

Santa Monica Pier, May 2014

What is the sea if not the swallower
of my lovelorn father? or so he threatened
after noting his sixty-seven-year-old hands,
hematoma beneath thin forearm skin,
loose jowl, mourning for the fifth time

that hour, *A man can only take so much
rejection.* As if I too were not hypnotized
by broken boats drifting abyssal, spears of light
dulling in the depths. Each decade warps
the wood pier further, brings forth another busker

with a Whitmanesque beard. Beside us
lie six silver fish vacant-eyed
on a built-in table, two knives
parallel to their stomachs,
the fisherman washing his hands.

Marriott Hotel, Marina del Rey

Crimson and mazarine,
the lobby's rug reminded me
of busted lips, peculiar

welts on a mouth's petals,
when you stopped your swagger
with a sneaker squeak

beside a planter, stuck
your thin arms behind you
like wings, and bent

your whole face into a white lily.
How could I not still love you,
even after your knife bloomed

my mother's chest, even after
your fist split your new partner's lip
into a blued canyon? Terrible

man, your face awash in pollen, crushed
ochre stuck to glasses frames
and nose hairs, your hands rubbing it

deeper into eyebrows, raining orange
dust down your white shirt, staining
yourself the color of sunset, dear

father, dear terrible man,
thank the lilies
for my tenderness.

Among the Things I Haven't Asked My Father Because I Love Him

1. When the cat spun from arms to wall, did you speak to him like a person? Were you sorry?
2. How did it feel to dump your baby son through a front door? Did neighbors see you? Were cars driving by?
3. Of all the punishments, why the family dogs? Twice?
4. What was harder, being unwanted by your mother or disowning your daughter?
5. Did you pay someone to burn the house down? Did you make peace with the boulders you placed, the trim you painted? Did you remember that one winter day, that one winter hour, when the concrete was iced & I skated & you filmed & just then: joy?
6. In prison did they pummel you for kicks, kick you for giggles?
7. What was worse, laughter or tears? Right before you'd attack, I mean.
8. Did you suspect cops would come round up your stolen gifts? Did you know I'd hug that stereo mid-song, so adoring was I of this special present from my dad?
9. What made you love us with such radiant eyes? Who taught you to treasure us like that? What light do you hide inside you, & where does it go when it goes?

Philadelphia

I don't know anymore the line between witness
and cruelty, whether you should see what I will
show you, the black magic of a shadow
gaining contour in the flickering streetlight,
19th Street just south of Fairmount, city of—
need I say it?—brotherly love. A man curled
on a sidewalk, slacks pulled down mid-thigh,
ass bare. In the flickering streetlight, 19th Street,
ass bare and opened, it seemed, by a nearby
broomstick, reddened raw by, maybe, the friction
of that opening opened long enough that the hole
remained open, like a tunnel, the softest cave
a man carries, maybe, the quietest mouth
a man speaks with, sleeping on a sidewalk,
a splinter maybe worn through his delicate
anal skin—and he was breathing, reader,
I can tell you that.

In the Middle Of

Philadelphia tonight is a constellation
of hospitals: drips & beeps & masked
mortals who smooth gloved hands
just so on this one's shoulder, pinch
a catheter with breath held *two-three-four*,
commas amid rows of respiratored strangers.
Earlier, Melinda walked borrowed dogs.
Patrick cheered out three windows
for the toddler inching her red tricycle.
In the middle of the Ave, neighbors traded
tablespoons of yeast for pints of vodka
sneakered above still cobblestones. I used to
lie, at 11 or 13, on the white striped crosswalk,
asphalt still warm from Los Angeles sun.
The sky beyond blinding streetlights
would wink its few stars—

Another Woman Shoved Down to the Gravel

I am tired of being small, not hiking
the Wissahickon's capillaries for fear—
another woman shoved down to the gravel
just last week. She got away.

One day I'll hoist over the park's
stone walls. Been building
toward unassisted pull-ups, dreaming
of lifting into trees above the trails.

I don't know that I could get away.
I don't know that I could recite my
Clifton, Hopkins, or Rich
behind grit teeth, panicked eyes.

But these arms—if they could punch
as they write, if they could launch me
into branches overhead, I might
never stop climbing, might never be

slaughtered in the woods, my head stuffed
with other people's poems, all the words
I never got to writing.

Miriam, I remember

that August, muggy St. Louis,
when sleepless on stab-springed daybed, I crept,
3 a.m., for beer. Aging bare bulb that flickered & dimmed,
you hunched over letters, lithium-drugged, wavy hair cropped,
shoes strapped, nerves jilting shoulders
below hum-mumble & tongue click.

Two decades, I'd daydreamt your upright piano,
your feet for running everywhere,
your typing fingers,
your squeal of a laugh,
your loud tears,
your bruised arms,
your *I never wanted your father*—
what you never quite called rape.

Miriam, years later, at the dying facility
off the Missouri county highway,
when you remembered
nothing of your luscious body
or how faucets work
or your lightning words,
but you finally saw me,

loved me with my name,
all the fallow bells in me
scorched peals through my veins—

       so fuck poisoned tongues, bipolar
     legacy; to hell with gnarled memory, gritted
   agony; goddamn violence, volatility, prescribed peace.
  Your eyes sang me the churned sweet
of gentle release,
   & mine sang back, holy grandmother, bone-rattled heat.

Berth

After his mother died, my dad crossed
his arms for two months,
lay still in his v-berth, pallid, living
off Fig Newtons and orange juice,
his mind a looped clip of her
pine box cranked down into earth,
his toes curling as he remembered
how we all shoveled, one by one, heaps
of heavy wet dirt over her dead
centered star.

At Framwellgate Bridge

Voices lap with the river,
   refining my city-growl ear
     as the Wear gleams in sunset.

Like his last letter, crumpled
   in my back pocket, my father
     wears away in his distance.

My eyes follow wings
   that dart and spin
     above smaller wings.

Father bird carries me
   to roofs and trees,
     lingers amid leaves,

flapping without flying.
   His feathers float down
     like dropped promises—

I came for this: to witness
   his set glare, his
     dive beneath the Wear.

This is not good-
   bye, but I release him
     as the ripples even.

5

Poem to My Therapist about the Abyss

Between sessions my Ferris wheel turns backward,
against time, & drowned selves surface like murky fish,

little Darlas barely glimpsed as night darkens the pier
over which the wheel spins. I once spun a few lunch breaks

on this wheel's cool plastic seats, a girlfriend or grief
saddled beside me. The ocean spread before us

like glittered marble crushed my lungs: I'd never be
whole. Whole parts of ourselves cower, traumas our bodies

bury, as mine did, I'd thought, years before Santa Monica
reopened the bright wheel my mind revisits when anxious,

& when I wrangle memory into phrases like *hurling telephone*,
like *nest of yanked hair*, & when I holler for the conductor to halt,

you remind me—*breathe, ground*—that beyond the dazzling wheel
are the wide worn slats of the pier my bare feet have walked,

the end of which is the same ocean as from above, but up close:
fish bodies darting: white queenfish, silver surfperch birthing

live fish from their own miraculous flesh: deep blue light
& shadow weaving through currents: a whole body of salt-licked bodies

alive & determined to live, all the way to the unfathomable depths
I once called *abyss*.

Still Trying

A child stomps in galoshes,
hops at the hover and swish
of European Herring

Gulls triumphant with silvery fish.
But the giddy girl's a gull
Irish stepdancing,

stomping Ogunquit Beach
for worms. Tired of swooping
and prancing, the gull

seems to believe
life will rise
because she stomps her foot.

Dear One

When we slow dance through the house,
   the rug scratches our feet, its borrowed
     fibers reminders of all we do not own—

and what does it matter? We have you.
   Kneaded bread dough never smelled
     this good—not even baking or cooling

into its crust. Down never felt this warm,
   not even in February's blizzard
     when we sweated our love beneath it.

Child, you have made this afternoon
   as sweet as life can be.
     The sun lights our calves

like citrine, our hair like cosmos,
   our eyes like caramel glaze. You,
     in your real flesh, pudgy arms

and slick round lips, are a vision
   we believe, the ether
     to which we cleave.

Poem for Evelyn

1.

Amid Brazilian samba drummers
      Philadelphia airport

      bodies signs stomps shouts

you fleshed my voice
                from within

        say it loud   say it clear
        refugees are welcome here

Your family too escaped terror
      once

      landed in New York & Texas

but your genes already know this

      lime-sized fetus   translucent skin
          nail buds just forming

2.

Your new voice warms this Philly treetop apartment
  while California burns Wars abroad
  veer again into morose

  radio drone

Four months old, anxious to stand, your feet
  cut air will soon

  attract bees & butterflies & mosquitoes

Do you hear the racket—drills,
  delivery trucks, leaf-blowers growling?

  You giggle under then over the machinery,
  rattles fisted

3.

After the molester president won,
    I stripped anyway,
        blue jeans crumpled,

feet stirruped, doctorly small talk, some blooming
    flower painting eye level,
        reclined
        anyway,

conceived you anyway,
    swayed the joyful nauseated hours
        for months,

& we marched January raw, pink,
    your cells proliferating flesh
        all winter

4.

When cracks a gunshot at dusk,
the mothers stiffen   skull to sacrum

Even when cops copter that way, downhill,
our babies cradled here, we panic—

cherry blood   spattering light post,
were not you too my child?

5.

Will you captain
> the old schooner,

celestial navigator? Drop anchor
> over NY subway car reefs

housing sea bass, mussels, & mackerel
> to check if green still blankets steel?

Will you pilot a tanker hauling guns
> to be recycled into beams

for schools, churches? Will you dive
> your someday middle-

aged body toward other wreckages, child?

When your body writes its poems,
> we, your mothers, we will sail with you

6.

& the mothers go back, go back
        Mine shoulders the Pacific
                corroding
        the underside of her house

Under her white living room,
        those dolphin-dappled waters
                carve your two mothers out also—
        the swirling plastics, the Syrian boats—

7.

    Gather these oceans   sandpiper
        bamboo coral   loggerhead anemone   right whale
nursing her young   Gather icebergs   Styrofoam-
        crested waves   Gather
dories & cruise ships   tugboats & schooners
        Gather phytoplankton & seaweed
ribboning across beaches   the last seals
        basking   Gather moon pull   tide lick
sunset blazing pastels that shush the sky
        Gather the sky where it kisses your face
Gather your face   where your mothers
        & theirs & theirs before kiss back through you
Gather the mothers through the air & we
        ocean you   & those you someday will birth too

8.

This late December day stretches
pink to orange to cerulean blue

To think I opened my body
for you just last summer,

Evelyn,

a push like three hurricanes & then

: soft wet head,
long arms

across my bare chest

Your lavender blue gray eyes
squinted

God, I said to you,
take this breath & sing

Notes

Pigs That Ran Straightaway into the Water, Triumph Of
    See Matthew 8:32 & the Mountain Goats song. Shout-out to Cara Armstrong.

Poem with First Line by Jean Valentine
    See Valentine's poem "Annunciation." With gratitude to Anne Marie Macari for this writing prompt & to Lee Ann Sporn, whose painting, *Water Striders*, responds to my poem.

I Tell Anne Sexton about My Uterus
    With gratitude to Carl Rubino, whose photographic diptych, "All Is Not What at First It Appears to Be," responds to this poem.

Ferning
    The microscopic examination of a woman's saliva & cervical fluids right before ovulation reveals the pattern of fern fronds. "Forty-one" playfully increases the Bible's forty years or days, depending on the story—a spiritual time of waiting & of faith for Moses, the Israelites, Jesus, etc.

Little Blue
    Several brands of pregnancy tests reveal a second line, often blue, to indicate pregnancy.

Still Trying
    European Herring Gulls stomp the ground rapidly to surface earthworms.

Poem to My Therapist about the Abyss
    With gratitude to watercolorist Catharine Moore, whose painting, *Circle of Life*, was created in conversation with my poem.

Gratitude

I first became a poet when my mother, Barbara Ann, taught me how to read in my childhood bedroom in Dallas: with patient repetition & playful attention to the phonic patterns & contextual meanings of language, she, my first teacher, instilled in me her own mother's love of reading. She encouraged me in all things but especially in reading & writing, & her strength, boundless love, perseverance, & intelligence were my childhood's greatest gifts. My father, Charles, also modeled passionate curiosity & wonder in general but most memorably while reading, dictionary close at hand on its sturdy wood stand. My parents' love of literature & language gave me a path I could trust, eventually writing my way here. To my siblings, Vanessa & Darren, & my nephew Miles, thank you for your loving companionship along the way.

The oldest of these poems came to life when I was a community college student enrolled, for the second time, in Mario Réne Padilla's poetry workshop, where I learned that poems, like people, are bolstered by community. The most recent was written seventeen years later, during a global pandemic, soon after defending my doctoral dissertation in a Zoom room with so many of my beloved community present via video. To all who have honored my life & writing with your presence before, during, or after these times, thank you.

I am especially grateful to the poet friends & mentors who helped me deepen these poems, with special gratitude to Maxine Kumin, Michael Waters, Mihaela Moscaliuc, Anne Marie Macari, Gerald Stern, Jean Valentine, Joan Larkin, Ross Gay, Alicia Ostriker, Patrick Rosal, Aracelis Girmay, Kathleen Sheeder Bonanno, Carol Muske-Dukes, Ira Sadoff, Jane Mead, Judith Vollmer, Lisa Alexander, Roberto Carlos Garcia, Yesenia Montilla, Lynne McEniry, David Crews, Lori Wilson, Elliott batTzedek, Cara Armstrong, Sosha Nicole Pinson, Sean Morrissey, Joe Shin, JC Todd, Monica Hand, Charles Manis, Michelle Greco, Jim Spears, Rebecca Gayle Howell, Peter Kirn, Shaun Fletcher, Mary Brancaccio, Brett Haymaker, Laurie Ann Guerrero, & Ellen Doré Watson.

Elizabeth Catanese, thank you for reading every draft of these poems with generosity & insight, & thank you for the myriad ways you nourish my life. Thank you to Melissa Orner & Ann Brown for being family. Thank you to Gloria Willis for believing in me all these years & for our rare friendship. What fortune to have you all in my life.

I'm also grateful to the Catanese clan at large (Mary Carol, Paul, Escher, & Dylan), Atsuko Tsuji, Nico Anwandter, Robin Becker, Holly Perry, Lana Gold, Elizabeth Lachman, Alex Lamm, Andy Chase, Lauren Sahl, Lily Chase, Ann Cleveland, Elizabeth Kim, Stephen Kelly, Vanessa Loh, Holly Raymond, Talissa Ford, Josh Lukin, Rachael Groner, Marcy Boroff, Maria Veneziano, Darah Lerner, Laura Whitman, Jackie Gutmann at RMA Philadelphia, Arts by the People, Get Fresh Books, kitties Addie & Whitman, & the greater web of wonders who hold space for me & my work, including you.

Last but never least, Betsy & Evelyn, you make me the luckiest person I've ever met. Thank you.

www.ingramcontent.com/pod-product-compliance
Lightning Source LLC
Chambersburg PA
CBHW081157070526
44583CB00021B/2878